My Amazing Body
BREATHING

Angela Royston

www.raintreepublishers.co.uk
Visit our website to find out more information about **Raintree** books.

To order:
- ☎ Phone 44 (0) 1865 888112
- 🖶 Send a fax to 44 (0) 1865 314091
- 🖥 Visit the Raintree bookshop at **www.raintreepublishers.co.uk** to browse our catalogue and order online.

First published in Great Britain by Raintree,
Halley Court, Jordan Hill, Oxford OX2 8EJ,
part of Harcourt Education.
Raintree is a registered trademark of Harcourt
Education Ltd.

Editorial: Nick Hunter and Catherine Clarke
Design: Kim Saar and Roslyn Broder
Illustrations: Will Hobbs
Picture Research: Maria Joannou and Pete Morris
Production: Jonathan Smith

Originated by Dot Gradations Ltd
Printed and bound in China by South China
Printing Company

ISBN 1 844 43383 8
08 07 06 05 04
10 9 8 7 6 5 4 3 2 1

British Library Cataloguing in Publication Data
Royston, Angela
Breathing. - (My Amazing Body)
612.2
A full catalogue record for this book is available from
the British Library.

Acknowledgements
The publishers would like to thank the following
for permission to reproduce photographs:
Alamy Images pp. **5**, **14** (Tony Charnock), **28**; Bubbles
p. **7**; Corbis pp. **6**, **16**, **19**, **24**, **26**, **27** (Stephen Frink);
FLPA pp. **9** (Gerard Lacz), **13** (Tony Wharton), **15** (Ron
Austing); **21** (Minden Pictures); NHPA (G. I. Bernard)
p. **17**; Pete Morris pp. **10**, **12**; Photofusion p. **22**
(Christa Stadtler); Science Photo Library pp. **4** (BSIP,
Vero/Carlo), **8** (Scott Camazine
and Sue Trainor), **18** (CNRI), **23** (A.B. Dowsett), **25** top
(Matt Meadows, Peter Arnold Inc.), **25** bottom (Matt
Meadows, Peter Arnold Inc.).

Cover photographs of an X-ray of the human chest
showing the lungs reproduced with permission of
Science Photo Library (BSIP, S&I) and child swimming
underwater reproduced with permission of Alamy
Images (SAMI SARKIS).

The publishers would like to thank Carol Ballard
for her assistance in the preparation of this book.

Every effort has been made to contact copyright
holders of any material reproduced in this book. Any
omissions will be rectified in subsequent printings if
notice is given to the publishers.

The paper used to print this book comes from
sustainable resources.

Contents

Any words appearing in bold, **like this**, are explained in the Glossary.

Inside and out

All living things breathe. They breathe for the same reason – to take in a **gas** called **oxygen.** Living things need oxygen to stay alive. People and other animals that live on land take in oxygen from the air. Animals that live in water take in oxygen from the water.

trachea

lungs

When you breathe in, air passes through your nose or mouth into a wide tube called the trachea, which leads to your lungs.

Breathing in air

Air is pulled into your body through your nose or your mouth. When you take a deep breath, you can feel the air going up your nose. You can also see your chest swell as the air is pulled into your **lungs.**

Humans cannot breathe in water. Before you jump in, you take a deep breath of air to keep you going while you are underwater.

Animals breathe too

Many land animals also breathe in air through nostrils or through their mouth, although the shape of their nose or mouth is often very different from ours. These animals, however, all have lungs that work like ours.

Why I need to breathe

Without **oxygen**, people and animals die within minutes. Every part of your body uses oxygen to stay alive and to keep working.

Muscles burn oxygen

You use your **muscles** to move your arms, legs and other parts of your body. Your muscles are like the engine of a car. A car engine uses oxygen to burn petrol to make the car wheels turn. In the same way, your muscles use oxygen to get energy from food.

This boy and his dog are using their muscles to run around. Their muscles use oxygen, from the air in their lungs, to get the energy to move.

Breathing out

Breathing out is just as important as breathing in! The **stale** air that you breathe out contains the **gases carbon dioxide** and **water vapour**. They are produced by the muscles and all other parts of the body as they work. Your body gets rid of these waste gases when you breathe out.

Thin air

The higher you are up a mountain the more often you have to breathe. This is because the air contains less oxygen than the air lower down.

The air that you breathe out makes a mist on a cold day. This is because it contains more water than the air around you.

Breathing in

You breathe in air through your nose or mouth. Either way, the air goes into a large, strong tube called the **trachea.**

Inside your nose

The part of your nose that you can see contains two channels called nostrils. Air goes up the nostrils and into the nasal passages inside your nose.

nose

mouth

throat

Most of your nose is inside your head. Both your nose and mouth lead to your throat.

There is more of your nose inside your head than on the outside! Your nasal passages are lined with mucus and fine hairs to catch any specks of dirt in the air you breathe in. If the air is cold, it warms up as it travels through your nose to reach your **throat**.

No noses

A bird is one kind of animal that does not have a nose. Instead it has two nostrils just above its beak.

Animal noses

Animals have different shapes of noses. Most dogs have long noses, although some, such as Pekineses, have short noses. Pigs have round snouts and an elephant has such a long nose (trunk) it can use it to lift logs.

An elephant uses its trunk to breathe and to sniff out food, water and danger.

Where the air goes

Air travels through your **trachea** and into breathing tubes, called bronchi. These tubes branch into narrower and narrower tubes inside your **lungs**.

Blowing out

When you blow out, you push extra air out of your lungs. No matter how hard you blow, you cannot empty your lungs completely.

When you breathe in, tiny bubbles in your lungs fill up with air, just like this balloon is filling with air.

Inside your lungs

The narrow tubes in your lungs end in tiny bubbles. When you breathe in, the bubbles stretch and fill with air. The walls of the bubbles are so thin that **oxygen** from the air passes through them into your blood. At the same time, **carbon dioxide** and **water vapour** pass from your blood into your lungs.

trachea

air in

air out

spine

ribs

diaphragm

breathing in

breathing out

You use your diaphragm and the muscles between your ribs to breathe in and out.

Taking a breath

A sheet of **muscle** below your lungs, called the **diaphragm**, helps you breathe in and out. When the diaphragm tightens, it makes space inside your lungs. Air rushes in to fill the space and, at the same time, muscles pull your **ribs** outwards. Then the diaphragm relaxes and your ribs move in, pushing some air out of the lungs.

Huffing and puffing

When you exercise hard, you soon begin to huff and puff. You breathe through your mouth to gulp in more air, and you breathe more quickly.

More oxygen

Exercise makes your **muscles** work much harder than usual. This means that they need extra **oxygen** to get extra energy. Your body tells you to breathe faster and deeper. The more you breathe, the more air goes into your **lungs** and the more oxygen goes into your blood.

When you're 'out of breath' you huff and puff to get more oxygen into your body.

Horses breathe harder when they gallop but they breathe the extra air out through their nostrils.

Getting rid of waste

At the same time, you blow out more **stale** air. This stale air contains the extra **water vapour** and **carbon dioxide** made by your hard-working muscles. When you stop to rest, your breathing quickly returns to normal.

Panting

Most animals cannot breathe through their mouths, so they do not huff and puff like humans do. Dogs pant, but usually to cool down, rather than to take in more air.

Breathing and exercise

You usually think of exercise making your **muscles** stronger, but exercise that makes you huff and puff, such as running, dancing, aerobics and even running up stairs, also makes your heart and **lungs** work better too.

Sprinters are the fastest runners over a short distance. Top sprinters run 100 metres on one breath of air!

Fastest animals

Cheetahs are the fastest animals, but they cannot sprint a long way. Antelopes can escape from cheetahs because they can keep running for longer.

Exercising your lungs

When you exercise, you breathe more deeply. The muscle below your lungs has to work harder to pull the extra air in. If you exercise regularly, you become more fit and can breathe more deeply without getting puffed out.

Exercising your heart

When you exercise, your heart beats faster. This sends more blood to your lungs to pick up extra **oxygen**. It also sends more blood and oxygen to your muscles. When you are fit, your heart works better – it pumps more blood with each beat without having to beat faster.

Breathing underwater

People and most land animals cannot breathe underwater. Although water contains **oxygen**, your body cannot take in oxygen from water. Instead you have to hold your breath when you swim underwater, or use special breathing equipment.

You can see the bubbles of stale air this diver has breathed out.

Swimming underwater

Using a snorkel is one way of breathing when your face is underwater. You breathe through a pipe that sticks out above the water. Divers that go deep underwater, carry a tank of special air with them. A breathing tube connects the tank to their mouth.

A fish's gills work like our lungs. Oxygen moves through them into the fish's blood.

Gills

Fish and shellfish breathe using their **gills**. They take in water through their mouth and push it out through their gills. As the water flows over the gills, oxygen moves from the water into the fish's blood.

A breath of air

Some sea animals cannot breathe underwater. Sea **mammals,** such as whales and seals, have **lungs** and have to come to the surface to breathe in air.

Speaking and singing

You can speak or sing as you breathe out. The noises that make words and sounds are made either in your mouth or **throat**. Many animals make sounds too, but they cannot speak as we do.

Forming sounds

Your larynx (or voice box) is at the top of your **trachea**. It contains two bands, or **vocal cords**. When you breathe in, the cords are relaxed so the air just passes through them.

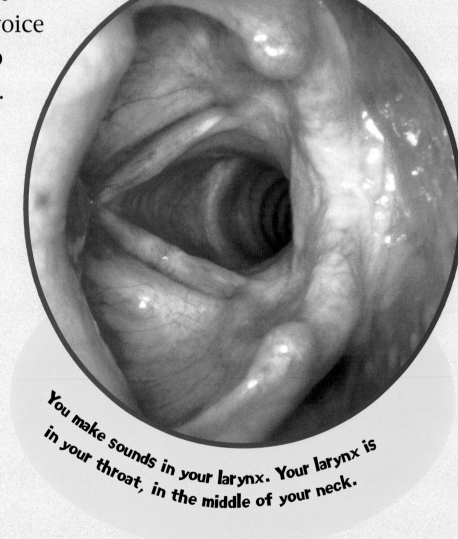

You make sounds in your larynx. Your larynx is in your throat, in the middle of your neck.

Animal sounds

Many animals have a larynx and make their own kind of sound. Some squeak, some others croak, bark or howl. Many birds sing using a wide range of notes.

To make different sounds, you tighten the cords as you breathe out. The cords **vibrate** in a different way for each sound. If you put your fingers on your throat as you speak or sing, you will feel the cords vibrating.

Making words

You can make many different notes using your larynx. To make words, you move your tongue and lips. Some sounds involve touching your teeth with your tongue.

When you sing you take a deep breath and use your larynx to make notes.

Hiccuping and yawning

It is hard to stop yourself hiccuping or yawning. You hiccup when your **lungs** draw in a short, sharp breath of air. Yawning is almost the opposite, you slowly draw in an extra big breath of air.

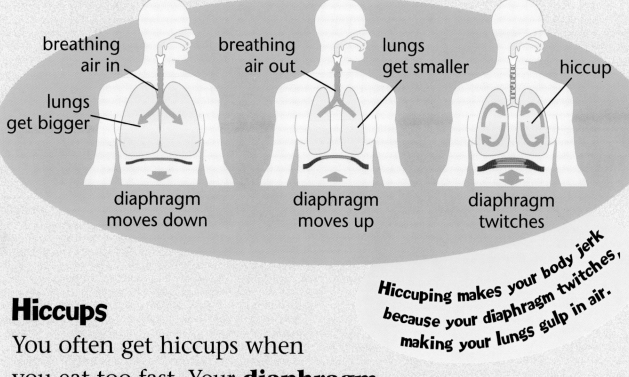

breathing air in

lungs get bigger

diaphragm moves down

breathing air out

lungs get smaller

diaphragm moves up

hiccup

diaphragm twitches

Hiccuping makes your body jerk, because your diaphragm twitches, making your lungs gulp in air.

Hiccups

You often get hiccups when you eat too fast. Your **diaphragm** usually tightens and relaxes gently as you breathe in and out, but sometimes it suddenly jerks, pulling in a gulp of air. As the air rushes in, a flap called the epiglottis closes over your **vocal cords**, making the 'hic' sound.

Yawning

You yawn when your brain is short of **oxygen,** perhaps when you are in a warm room or when you are tired or bored. Yawning pulls more air, and so more oxygen, into your body. Some of the oxygen goes to your brain to make you more alert.

Many animals and people yawn when they wake up. Yawning helps to make the brain more alert.

Curing hiccups

There are lots of ideas about how to stop hiccups, including holding your breath or drinking water from the far side of a cup.

Sneezing and coughing

Sneezing and coughing are ways of clearing your nose and the airways into and inside your **lungs**. Both sneezing and coughing send a blast of air out of your body.

Sneezing

You sneeze when something **irritates** the inside of your nose. Breathing in dust or pepper, for example, can make you sneeze. Some people are **allergic** to pollen from plants and other fine dust, which make them sneeze.

When you sneeze or cough, air rushes out of your body as fast as a car on the motorway!

22

Coughing

You catch a cold when you breathe in certain **germs**. Colds, allergies and **asthma** all create extra **mucus** that can block the narrow airways inside your lungs. Extra mucus also blocks the tubes into your lungs. Coughing helps to loosen the mucus and clear the tubes.

This photo shows what one of the germs that causes colds looks like when it is magnified thousands of times.

Dust bath

An elephant doesn't sneeze when it sucks dust into its trunk. Instead it blows the dust over its skin to get rid of ticks and mites.

What can go wrong?

When you have a cold, your body makes extra **mucus**, which can block your nose and breathing tubes. While the cold lasts, you may find breathing difficult.

Asthma

People who have **asthma** often find it difficult to breathe. During an asthma attack, the narrow tubes in their **lungs** become tight and swollen. People with asthma usually carry an inhaler, which produces a vapour they breathe in. The vapour relaxes the tubes, making it easier to breathe.

This boy is breathing in through an inhaler to relieve an asthma attack.

Smoking tobacco

People who smoke tobacco breathe in hot smoke that burns their **throat** and lungs. Tobacco smoke contains black, sticky tar. If a person smokes regularly, tiny specks of tar collect in their lungs and block their narrow tubes. Over a long time, smoking can cause **cancer**.

Even if you do not smoke, other people's tobacco smoke can damage your lungs. The smoke **irritates** the lining of the tiny tubes in your lungs, making you cough.

The lung at the top is healthy, but the dirty, damaged lung at the bottom belonged to a smoker.

Healthy breathing

It is healthier to breathe in fresh air, than to breathe in stuffy, **stale** air. Fresh air contains more **oxygen** and helps to keep your brain alert.

Breathe through your nose

It is better to breathe through your nose than through your mouth. Hairs and **mucus** inside your nose catch most of the dust and **germs** that you breathe in.

Fresh air is good for your lungs. It contains more oxygen and fewer germs than stale air.

Breathtaking record

Sperm whales dive deep underwater, holding their breath, for more than an hour. At the surface, whales breathe through a blow hole on top of their head. They blow out spouts of stale air and **water vapour** as they breathe out.

Your breathing tubes are also lined with tiny hairs and mucus. They catch any specks of dust and germs that get past your nose, and push them back up the tubes to keep them clear.

Breathe deeply

When you breathe deeply, more of the tiny bubbles in your lungs fill with air. Hold your breath and then breathe out slowly. Exercising your lungs like this will help them to work better.

The whole body

Different parts of your body rely on each other to work properly. Your body is made up of millions of different **cells**. Every cell in your body uses **oxygen** that comes from the air you breathe into your **lungs**. All the cells in your breathing system need food to stay alive and keep working.

The food you eat provides fuel so all the cells in your body can keep working.

Fuel

Fuel comes from the food you eat, but before your cells can use it, it has to be **digested** by your stomach and intestines. It then passes into your blood and is carried around your body.

Controlling breathing

Your brain controls your whole body. The part of the brain that controls breathing usually works without you thinking about it. Your brain signals to your **diaphragm** every few seconds to make you breathe in. You can, however, think about your breathing and make yourself breathe more slowly or faster.

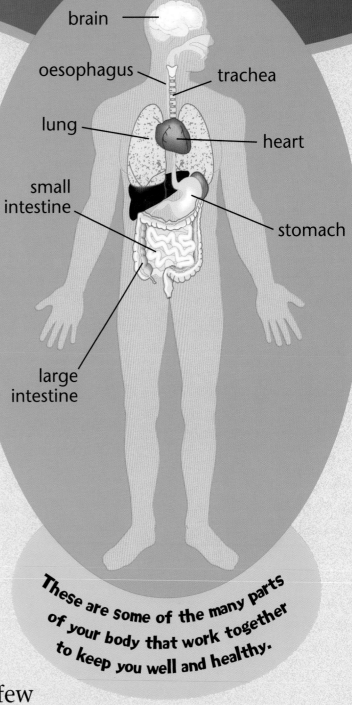

brain

oesophagus

trachea

lung

heart

small intestine

stomach

large intestine

These are some of the many parts of your body that work together to keep you well and healthy.

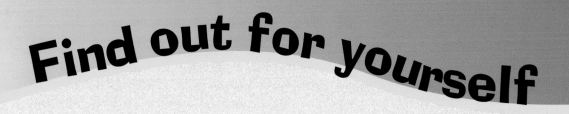

Find out for yourself

Everybody's body is slightly different but they all work in the same way. Find out more about how your own amazing body works by noticing what happens to it. How long can you run before you get out of breath? When do you yawn, and does it make you feel more awake? What makes you sneeze and cough? You will find the answers to many of your questions in this book, but you can also use other books and the Internet.

Books to read

Why do I sneeze? and other questions about breathing, Angela Royston (Heinemann Library, 2002)

Your Body: Breathing, A. Sandeman (Franklin Watts, 2000)

Body Works: Breathing, Paul Bennett (Belitha Press, 1998)

Using the Internet

Explore the Internet to find out more about breathing. Websites can change, but if some of the links below no longer work, don't worry. Use a search engine, such as www.yahooligans.com or www.internet4kids.com, and type in keywords such as 'breathing', '**lungs**' and '**asthma**'.

Websites:

www.kidshealth.org contains lots of information about how your body works and how to stay healthy

www.bbc.co.uk/science/humanbody/body contains an interactive body and lots of information. Click on 'lungs' and 'voice box' to find out more about breathing and speaking.

www.asthma.org.uk/kidszone contains information about asthma and how to deal with it.

Disclaimer
All the Internet addresses (URLs) given in this book were valid at the time of going to press. However, due to the dynamic nature of the Internet, some addresses may have changed, or sites may have ceased to exist since publication. While the author and publishers regret any inconvenience this may cause readers, no responsibility for any such changes can be accepted by either the author or the publishers.

Glossary

allergic when your body reacts to something as though it were a germ, even though that thing is harmless to most people

asthma condition that makes it hard to breathe in and out

cancer disease in which some cells in the body begin to grow out of control

carbon dioxide waste gas produced in the cells of your body that leaves your body in the air that you breathe out

cell smallest building block of living things

diaphragm large, flat muscle between your lungs and stomach that tightens and relaxes to let you breathe in and out

digest break up food into smaller pieces inside your body

gas substance that is not a liquid or a solid. Some gases, such as oxygen, are in the air we breathe.

germ tiny living thing that can make you ill

gill part of the body that an animal that lives underwater uses to take in oxygen

irritate make part of the body more sensitive

lungs parts of the body that take in oxygen when you breathe in and get rid of waste carbon dioxide and water vapour when you breathe out

magnify make something look much larger

mammal animal that feeds its babies with milk made inside the mother's body

mucus liquid that lines some tubes inside the body, such as your nostrils and breathing tubes

muscles parts of your body that you use to move

nasal passage passageway inside the nose

oxygen gas that living things need to breathe to survive

ribs bones in your chest that protect your lungs

stale used, or old

throat tube inside your neck that joins your mouth and nose to your lungs and stomach

trachea tube that leads from your throat to the bronchial tubes in your lungs

vibrate shake backwards and forwards very fast

vocal cords bands in your throat that tighten and relax to allow you to make different sounds with your voice

water vapour water in the form of a gas

Index

Raintree Perspectives version

Titles in the *My Amazing Body* series include:

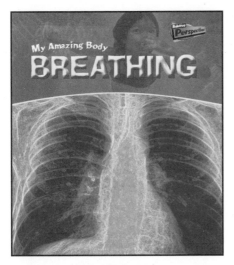

Hardback 1 844 43383 8

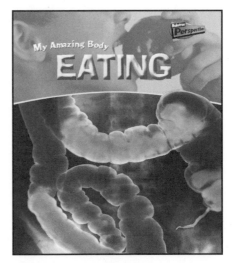

Hardback 1 844 43384 6

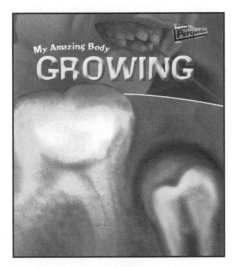

Hardback 1 844 43385 4

Hardback 1 844 43386 2

Hardback 1 844 43387 0

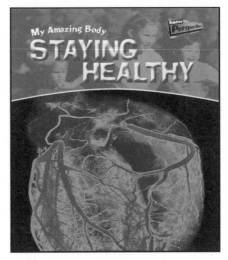

Hardback 1 844 43388 9

Find out about the other titles in this series on our website www.raintreepublishers.co.uk